ELL Teachers and Special Education

A Self-Study or Group Study

Created by Steve Gill and Ushani Nanayakkara

Introduction

This work came about through a series of different requests. First, a request was made by special education staff regarding helping our ELL partners to know more about special education issues. Steve then surveyed several hundred special education staff on what they wanted ELL teachers to learn about special education. Steve provided this information at the state bilingual educator conference (WABE). After presenting the information, Steve worked with the audience to create a list of questions regarding what they still wanted answered. Steve drafted answers to these questions and then had the answers vetted by numerous experts around the state. This information was posted on the WABE website. Finally, with the input from various stakeholders, the decision was made to create this self-study course.

The self-study consists of content modules, question and answer modules, scenario modules, and a resources page. In each of the modules you will be provided information or asked to reflect on your own knowledge, then you will be asked questions about the topic (a quiz), then you will be provided further information, finally you will be asked to reflect on the topic based upon what you knew and what you learned. This course is meant to be completed in the order presented. Please make sure to not skip forward, so that the process of what you know, what you learned, and what you still want to know will work effectively.

Steve Gill is a teacher, school psychologist, and the ESA Coach for the Kent School District. He works actively with many state associations and state department groups on ELL and Special Education topics, and has three books published in this area with his co-author (and wife) Ushani Nanayakkara.

Course Objectives

1) The learner will be able to describe key aspects of special education that will increase their knowledge in areas they will use within their job.
2) The learner will learn areas in which they need to research more deeply to be able to best serve their students.
3) The learner will be better able to describe key aspects of the special education process and how they can be an active partner during the process.

This course does:

1) Provide the learner a broad overview of the special education process.
2) Provide the learner ideas regarding ways in which they can actively participate in the process.
3) Provide the learner with questions taken directly from ELL staff and Special Education staff regarding what they want to know and be known.
4) Provide the learner with an opportunity to assess their knowledge, learn and reflect.
5) Provide the learner with real life scenarios and the types of problems/dilemmas they might face.

This course does not:

1) Replace your state law or district policy.
2) Go into depth in any one area of special education knowledge as it would for staff who spend each of their days working within special education processes or laws.
3) Answer all questions. Special Education and ELL are very complex fields that take years of study and experience to understand.

The hope of the authors for this course is that each and every learner will benefit from this course, be able to carry this knowledge forward into their daily practices, to understand where they need to learn more about ELL/Special Education issues, and enjoy themselves through what is hopefully an interesting learning experience.

Training Layout

Introduction (Modules 1 and 2)

<u>Module 1</u>

1) Why Special Education Qualification and Why Not Special Education Qualification?
2) Categories of Special Education Eligibility and Some Basics
3) Legal Information

<u>Module 2</u>

1) Language Learner Versus Student with a Disability Who Happens to be a Language Learner
2) Special Education and ELL Teachers Working Together
3) Characteristics of the Special Education Categories That Tend to Have Disproportionality Issues

Question and Answer Section (Modules 3, 4 and 5)

<u>Module 3:</u> The Referral Process

<u>Module 4:</u> The Evaluation Process

<u>Module 5:</u> Additional Questions and Answers on Varied Topics

Scenarios (Modules 6, 7, and 8)

<u>Module 6:</u> Student struggling to learn to read 1

<u>Module 7:</u> Student struggling to learn to read 2

<u>Module 8:</u> Student who has autism who happens to be an English language learner

Resources

There are not very many books written on this topic, nor research, nor articles, when compared to other educational topics. The list given here has books written or read by the authors that have been positively reviewed by many readers.

Please note: This course is designed to be completed in the order of the modules as described above.

Introduction - Module 1, Part 1

Why Special Education Qualification and Why Not Special Education Qualification?

The assumption is made that evaluating a student for special education services, qualifying them for special education services, and then delivering special education services cannot possibly be harmful to a child. Then, at times, the assumption is made that we cannot evaluate a student for special education services if they have not been in the country learning English for 3 years, or 5 years, or some other number that is incorrectly placed into this discussion.

The goal of the special education process is not to qualify students for special education, nor is it to keep students out of special education services, the goal is to identify correctly the students who need special education services.

Go to the next page after creating your answers.

Quiz

1) How does one know whether or not a student needs special education services?
2) What are two or more potential harmful impacts of evaluating and/or serving a student for special education who does not have a disability?
3) What is the core reason that holding off evaluating a student who truly has a disability (who would meet the special education eligibility requirements) is harmful?

Answer to question number 1: How does one know whether or not a student needs special education services?

A team of qualified professionals (e.g., school psychologist, special education teacher, speech/language pathologist) goes through a process that they have been trained to complete. This process has legal requirements (each of your states has a version of this that is based off the federal laws, in which your state can add to the federal laws, but not take away from the federal laws). The team tries to determine whether or not the student meets the criteria for one of the disability categories outlined in these laws, whether or not this disability has an adverse impact on the student's ability to access their education, and whether or not special education services are needed in order to address the adverse impact of the disability.

Answer to question number 2: What are two or more potential harmful impacts of evaluating and/or serving a student for special education who does not have a disability?

The parents and teachers of this student are going to have the impression that the student has a disability (see the research by Walter Gilliam, Yale University, to better understand the impact of impressions/biases on students). The student will likely be removed from their core instruction to receive the special education instruction for some portion of the day. Therefore, they will have less access to the core instructional time while receiving a service that they do not actually need. They will eventually (in many but not all cases) view themselves as someone with a disability in the noted areas and often view themselves as less able. The research on special education indicates that special education has a negative effect size (meaning it is not helping our children as a group). It is the opinion of this author that special education struggles to be of full benefit to the students it serves due to challenges with intensity of service. And, for each student who needs something other than special education (students incorrectly qualified), the ability of special education staff to provide needed intensity of service to the children who truly have a disability (that is negatively impacting their ability to access their education) is impacted negatively when the teachers have to split their time and effort (not always, obviously).

Answer to question number 3: What is the core reason that holding off evaluating a student who truly has a disability (who would meet the special education requirements) is harmful?

Special education is designed to ensure that students who have disabilities have services, specially designed instruction, accommodations, modifications and more to make sure they are accessing their core instruction to the best of their abilities. Delaying these services due to the difficulty of obtaining an accurate evaluation of language learners, or the difficulty caused by the short time they have been in the country learning English, is inappropriate and in some cases illegal. Would we delay a special education evaluation of a language learner if the language learner had blindness or deafness?

Reflections

Now that you have read the introduction to this section, taken the quiz, and read the answers, it is time to reflect.

1) What have you learned that is new information to you?
2) How will this change your work with students moving forward?
3) What do you still need to learn? Where will you find it? When will you find it?

Introduction - Module 1, Part 2

Categories of Special Education Eligibility and Some Basics

This starts out with a little bit of confusion. That is, the number of categories of eligibility for special education varies across the states, most being between 12 and 14. Although the federal law provides guidance on this, that is not helpful if it does not match your state information. The confusion is caused by the fact that some states combine visual impairments with blindness, some states combine hard of hearing with deafness, and some might combine both (the author has not seen this, but it is likely). The following is the list of categories straight from the Washington Administrative Code (WAC) as an example:

▶ **Areas of Eligibility (the categories)**

▶ Intellectual disability, a hearing impairment (including deafness), a speech or language impairment, a visual impairment (including blindness), an emotional behavioral disability, an orthopedic impairment, autism, traumatic brain injury, an other health impairment, a specific learning disability, deaf-blindness, multiple disabilities, or for students, three through eight, a developmental delay and who, because of the disability and adverse educational impact, has unique needs that cannot be addressed exclusively through education in general education classes with or without individual accommodations, and needs special education and related services.

▶ **WAC 392-172A-01035**

The good news for you as the student is that you really do not need to memorize this list of categories. If you need to know the list for your state, it is highly likely that a school psychologist or a speech/language pathologist will be able to provide you the correct list for your state.

The reasons why you really do not need to know all of these categories is that only a few of the categories are problematic for our language learners, some of these are very low incidence (so you might never work with a student with the noted disability). In many cases obtaining this information while you work with a student with the low incidence disability is more useful. Focusing in on a few categories, the ones that you are most likely to interact with, is the most useful approach.

Go to the next page after creating your answers.

Quiz

1) What are some of the categories that are less problematic regarding ELL/Special Education issues?
2) What are some of the categories that you have never heard about?
3) What categories are most problematic and can lead to questionable qualification issues with language learners?

Answer to Question 1: What are some of the categories that are less problematic regarding ELL/Special Education issues?

The categories that are usually the least problematic for language learners are the following: Hearing Impairment (including deafness), visual impairment (including blindness), orthopedic impairment, traumatic brain injury, deaf-blindness, and multiple disabilities. Depending upon your state, this could be one-half of the categories that you do not need to worry about as much. For some of these categories, not speaking English has little or no relationship to whether or not special education services are needed (e.g., blindness or deafness). For some of these categories, the students are extremely rare and you are very unlikely to interact with them (e.g., deaf-blindness).

Answer to Question 2: What are some of the categories that you have never heard about?

It is likely that many readers have not heard about the category of traumatic brain injury (often referred to as TBI). The category 'multiple disabilities' is a category that many people think of logically, but might not have known that it is an actual category.

Answer to Question 3: What categories are most problematic and can lead to questionable qualification issues with language learners?

The following categories are the categories with the greatest quantity of disproportionality, indicating they are the categories with the most problems for our language learners: specific learning disability, speech or language impairment, and developmental delay. The category of specific learning disability is problematic for our native English speakers (over identification or incorrect identification). Therefore, adding the aspects of language learning only makes the problems worse. For our students within the category of speech or language impairment, many of these students are being evaluated on components that either do not exist in their language or that they have not been exposed to educationally. For our students within the category of developmental delay, this is our younger students who are often missing needed exposure and/or experience. Therefore, the tests are not measuring a disability, but instead a lack of exposure and/or experience.

Reflections

Now that you have read the introduction to this section, taken the quiz, and read the answers, it is time to reflect.

1) What have you learned that is new information to you?
2) How will this change your work with students moving forward?
3) What do you still need to learn? Where will you find it? When will you find it?

Introduction - Module 1, Part 3

Legal Information

Each state takes the federal laws (CFR 300...) and uses these laws to create laws within that state. Each state has the ability to add to the federal laws, but cannot take away from the federal laws. Having read the federal laws and the laws for about 10 individual states, the norm is that states tend to add content based upon problems they are facing and trying to address.

You do not need to be an expert in your state special education laws, and the reality is that very few people reach a level of expertise in these laws without working with them on a daily basis (they are like a foreign language). You might want to begin by reading the material that your state provides to parents (most states have something that is referred to as "procedural safeguards" for parents). These are usually 40-50 pages and written with more explanation than the actual laws (which rarely have any explanation).

Given that the categories of Specific Learning Disability, Speech or Language Impairment, and Developmental Delay tend to be the categories with the most issues/problems for our language learners and the professionals trying to figure out how to determine between language acquisition and disability, these are likely the categories that you should examine first.

Go to the next page after creating your answers.

Quiz

1) How does a student qualify under the category of Specific Learning Disability?
2) What are two problems speech pathologists face when trying to determine whether a presenting issue(s) is a disability or language acquisition based?
3) What are two problems teams face when trying to determine if a presenting problem is a disability or not for our young children who might qualify under the category of developmental delay?
4) What do you know about the special education referral and evaluation process?

These are very complex issues and the following answers only touch on the surface of these issues. The answers given below are seen as covering the most commonly discussed areas.

Answer to Question 1: How does a student qualify under the category of Specific Learning Disability?

There are three common methods used to determine whether or not a student qualifies for special education services as a student with a specific learning disability. First, the discrepancy model. In a nutshell, this is a model in which a student is considered to have a disability if their measured IQ is significantly higher than their measured academic achievement. Second, the RTI (Response to Intervention) model. This is a model that states that if a student is given researched-based intervention and their response to the intervention (meaning their rate of growth in the intervention area) is much slower than their peers, they have a disability. Last, the Pattern of Strengths and Weaknesses model. This is a model in which the school psychologist looks at the patterns of strengths and weaknesses on the intelligence testing and compares that to strengths and weaknesses within the academic testing. If there are certain weaknesses within the intelligence testing that logically corresponds to weaknesses in academics, then the student has a disability.

It is important to note that in all cases (especially for language learners) the team is supposed to rule out issues related to the environment, culture, language learning, and whether or not the student had effective teaching in reading and math (something that is difficult to achieve if a student is being taught in a language they do not yet understand).

Answer to Question 2: What are two problems speech pathologists face when trying to determine whether a presenting issue(s) is a disability or language acquisition based?

The speech and language pathologists usually have very good information regarding the speech sounds, patterns, and normal development of students in English and Spanish. However, we have over 400 languages in our schools. Therefore, speech and language pathologists often struggle to determine developmental norms in a language (to understand if the student is demonstrating a problem that is relatively normal within that language). They also try to determine if the sound errors or struggles are due to the sound(s) (the one(s) needed in English) is/are not a sound(s) made in the native language of the student.

Answer to Question 3: What are two problems teams face when trying to determine if a presenting problem is a disability or not for our young children who might qualify under the category of developmental delay?

Young children are often over qualified. These children are children going through major life transitions, struggling with cultural issues, and whose parents often are under significant stress. They are expected to learn and behave in a manner that might not make any sense to them, nor their parents. For some of these children, their parents do not speak any English and are not literate in their native language. This can bring into the picture many issues for these students. For example, their parents might be working multiple jobs just to survive. Also, if one does not read in their native language, it is normal for the vocabulary to be smaller and less complex. As a result, the students have fewer words in which to use when transferring knowledge.

Answer to Question 4: What do you know about the special education referral and evaluation process? Provide as many details at you can.

The special education referral process is meant to be a period of time in which the team gathers data to determine whether or not to ask the parent(s) for written consent to evaluate their child for potential eligibility for special education services. The timeframe in which a team is allotted to gather this information and notify the parent of the decision (either to propose an initial evaluation or to refuse an initial evaluation) varies by state (your school psychologist can explain the timeframe within your state).

Anyone with knowledge of the student can make a special education referral and all referrals must be processed as dictated by your state laws. The parent must be notified in writing of the referral (even if they made the referral). Then the team begins to officially gather data on the student (additional data that is part of the referral process). This data should include historical information (like a review of the cumulative file and developmental information), current information (parent and teacher feedback about strengths and weaknesses), documentation of interventions tried and the results of these interventions. There are other things that can be included, given each student will present differently. Also, for our language learners, there are many more things to consider (there are books recommended in the resources section that cover this in more detail and later in this document you'll find more information).

Once the team believes that they have the needed data to make the appropriate decision, then the parents must be notified in writing of this decision. Sometimes there are meetings held during this process and sometimes there are not. There should always be meetings when the concerns of the individuals on the team and the data do not coincide well.

Reflections

Now that you have read the introduction to this section, taken the quiz, and read the answers, it is time to reflect.

Before answering these questions, if possible, take a few minutes to talk with your school psychologist and SLP regarding these questions and answers. You might come up with other answers that are valid answers.

1) What have you learned that is new information to you?
2) How will this change your work with students moving forward?
3) What do you still need to learn? Where will you find it? When will you find it?

Introduction - Module 2, Part 1

Language Learner Versus Student with a Disability Who Happens to Be a Language Learner

There are entire books written on this topic (several of which are mentioned in the resource section). The first and most important point is: there is no "test" that answers this question/dilemma. There are methods that help to increase the accuracy of testing, like those in the books written by Dr. Catherine Collier, Dr. Sam Ortiz, and me (Steve Gill). This information helps teams to make sure that they are gathering the most important information. Then, possibly even more important, there is guidance on how to examine the data that your team has gathered.

A component that is often missing in books on this topic is the importance of schools and/or districts evaluating the size of the problem within their school or district. For example, if a district completes an appropriate examination of their own data and finds out that their language learners are identified for each of the special education categories at roughly the same rate as their native English speakers; it is likely that the processes that they already have in place are working well. I have worked with over 200 school districts at this point, many of which have given me their data, and I have not seen a single district, not one, in which there was zero disproportionality. The problem of inappropriate identification of language learners is very wide spread.

The answers on the following page provide some insight into core aspects that must be examined.

<u>Go to the next page after creating your answers.</u>

Quiz

1) What are 5 key things to know about a language learner prior to discussing a special education referral?
2) What are the two main areas of disproportionality for language learners in your school/district?
3) What do you believe are 3 key factors for distinguishing between language learners who are having normal adjustment issues versus language learners who are students with disabilities?

Answer to question number 1: What are 5 key things to know about a language learner prior to discussing a special education referral?

There are a lot more than 5. I am choosing to provide you 10 with areas, many of them with their own set of questions. These are from the analysis matrix in our book listed in the resource section.

1) What languages are spoken in the home, who speaks each language, how much is each language spoken?
2) How many years of formal education did the student have in their native language? How did they do in school? How did their siblings or other relatives do in the same setting?
3) Are their parents literate in the languages spoken in the home? Are there written forms of the languages spoken in the home? Did the parents read to the children in these languages?
4) Did the student learn to read in their native language?
5) How many years have they been learning English?
6) How has their attendance history been?
7) What methodology does the school use for ELL services (e.g., pull-out, dual language)?
8) How does their progress on the state language acquisition test compare to like peers in your school?
9) How have they responded to targeted intervention in the area of concerns as compared to like peers in your school?
10) What are the expectations of the classroom teacher, school and parent(s) toward their learning?

These questions are just the tip of the iceberg, but they are questions that can lead to good discussions (if the right people are at the table), and those discussions can lead to better understanding the needs of the student.

Answer to question number 2: What are the two main areas of disproportionality for language learners in your school/district?

This is something that you will need to ask around to find out about. In reality, I would not be surprised if you are unable to actually obtain an answer. Then, one needs to ask themselves, "How do we solve a problem when we don't know where it starts nor how big it is?"

Any time in which you (anyone) are involved in a problem, there is a basic question that needs to be answered, "Are you part of creating, maintaining, or solving the problem?" Without knowing where the problem is, not knowing any of the data, how does a district or school begin to solve the problem?

If you are able to find an answer to this question, then the next logical question is, "What are we doing to solve this problem?" The resource books noted have information to assist in problem solving, either by providing information to increase understanding, providing steps in problem understanding/solving, or both.

Answer to question number 3: What do you believe are 3 key factors for distinguishing between language learners who are having normal adjustment issues versus language learners who are students with disabilities?

The following are what this author believes to be the three most important factors that begin the process of answering this question.

1) How did the student of concern perform on interventions that are targeted at the core problem, when compared to like peers?
2) Is there any evidence of the student having the same problem(s) in their native language? And/or the same problem in schooling in native language?
3) Is there a clear disability condition that is not linked to language acquisition?

There are many more factors that are truly critical, and the resource books noted assist in diving much deeper into this topic.

Reflections

Now that you have read the introduction to this section, taken the quiz, and read the answers, it is time to reflect.

1) What have you learned that is new information to you?
2) How will this change your work with students moving forward?
3) What do you still need to learn? Where will you find it? When will you find it?

Introduction - Module 2, Part 2

Special Education and ELL Teachers Working Together

Both special education services and ELL services are services, once a student qualifies, that legally must be delivered to the student (with some exceptions, for example, the parental right to revoke special education services). Therefore, if you work in an environment in which the student does not get one service or the other because someone believes that would be "double dipping" you need to question that response at length.

To get the best for our students, we need to work together. The core to this work is leveraging the knowledge of your colleagues. The norm is that special education staff are not as well educated on language acquisition issues/teaching and our ELL teachers are not as well educated on special education issues/teaching. You have the opportunity to learn more about how students with disabilities learn and effective teaching for students with disabilities. As you learn more about the methodologies and issues, keep in mind how ELL specific methodology can both fit in with and enhance what is already occurring. Think about what might be missing within the special education services that your language learner needs. Also, learn about the IEP process and how you can add benefit to the process, increasing the likelihood that your students will receive the most benefit from their services.

Go to the next page after creating your answers.

Quiz

1) What are two methodologies that you use in teaching language learners that might apply to increasing the special education services benefits for dually qualified students? And, how?
2) Have you seen or know of anything within special education that is similar to your ELL methodology? If you cannot answer this question, please take time to visit with the special education teacher in your building prior to moving on to the answers. After the visit, try to answer this question.
3) What can you do to integrate the two methodologies for your student?

Answer to question number 1 (there are many possible answers, this is just an example):

What are two methodologies that you use in teaching language learners that might apply to increasing the special education services benefits for dually qualified students? And, how?

The usage of realia or photos to link the vocabulary and discussion to meaningful information for the child. Total physical response is a second method that would apply.

In both of these cases, we are trying to make the input from our new language comprehensible to the students (instead of remaining abstract).

Answer to question number 2 (there are many possible answers, this is just an example):

Have you seen or know of anything within special education that is similar to your ELL methodology? If you cannot answer this question, please take time to visit with the special education teacher in your building prior to moving on to the answers. After the visit, try to answer this question.

For our students who are functioning at a higher level, we might be using books on tape so that they can read along while the story is read to them. We might also be using new technology that allows a student to snip a section on the computer screen and have it read to them. For our students who are lower functioning and/or who have communication problems, we might be using social stories or PECS (explained briefly below).

In all of these cases, we are trying to make the content more comprehensible for the student. In many of these cases the students have reading disabilities that limit (sometimes completely) their ability to get meaning from text, as though it was a language they do not know.

In both the ELL and special education examples, the goal is to make the information comprehensible (you might want to read more from Stephen Krashen, who coined the term comprehensible input within language learner instructional methodology, if you have not already done so). We want to remove as many barriers to understandings as possible, so that learning the core information is more accessible.

PECS is a system that uses pictures to help the student communicate their wants and needs.

Social Stories are a series of pictures that a teacher, therapist or school psychologist uses to teach a student a routine or and expectation (e.g., how to brush your teeth).

Answer to question number 3: What can you do to integrate the two methodologies for your student?

As the teacher of ELL students and as someone who has studied language learning, you can help the special education teacher better understand the stages of language learning. You can help the special education teacher understand the concepts of comprehensible input from the lens of a language learner. You might also be more familiar with the cultural issues that are occurring within the family and community, and help the special education teacher understand that certain behaviors can be related to cultural norms and/or struggles with issues related to having a student with a disability within that specific culture.

Reflections

Now that you have read the introduction to this section, taken the quiz, and read the answers, it is time to reflect.

1) What have you learned that is new information to you?
2) How will this change your work with students moving forward?
3) What do you still need to learn? Where will you find it? When will you find it?

Introduction - Module 2, Part 3

Characteristics of the Special Education Categories That Tend to Have Disproportionality Issues

The problems with disproportionality are significant in one category of special education, problematic in two categories of special education, and rare in over one half of the possible categories. That is, over one-half of the categories have little or no history of disproportionality. The answers on the next page will go into further detail, given the questions in the quiz are going to ask you to make some educated guesses.

The largest category of special education is the category of specific learning disability. This can be evaluated using the three primary methods noted earlier in this document. The point with these students is the belief that they have a disability in (usually) reading, math or writing skills. These disabilities are less "concrete" in nature, given that the staff cannot "see" something that creates the struggles the students face. Roughly 80% of all students within special education services have reading as a concern or an area of service. Then, there are many students who have a disability that is more concrete in nature. That is, students who have blindness, visual impairments, deafness, physical disabilities (the category can be orthopedic impairment within special education), or traumatic brain injuries.

Go to the next page after creating your answers.

Quiz

1) In module 1, part 3, all of the categories (as used in the WAC) are named. Using this, which 3 would you guess have the greatest degree of disproportionality? And, why?
2) Using the same list, which categories do you believe have very low rates of disproportionality? And, why?
3) Why could it be valuable to know what category a student qualifies within and to know more about that category of eligibility?

Answers to question number 1: In module 1, part 3, all of the categories (as used in the WAC) are named. Using this, which 3 would you guess have the greatest degree of disproportionality? And, why?

The categories with the greatest degree of disproportionality are: specific learning disability, speech or language impairment, and developmentally delayed.

The following is based upon working many years in this field and working with people across the country on these issues. There really is very little research that speaks to this issue. The reason why categories are over used is due to a multitude of factors, and the weight of each factor is not known. First, these are all students who are struggling to learn in their environment. Special education is a service in which schools receive extra money in order to provide extra services to the children. The educators are good and caring people who believe they are doing the best that they can for the student(s) and that an incorrect classification as a student with a disability is harmless (which is not true). Second, there are staff members who truly believe that these students have disabilities and are often unaware that they are qualifying one specific group as students with disabilities at a much higher rate than any other group. It is actually rare that a district knows their own data in this area at any true level of depth.

"ELL students in schools that do not have an "RTI" model in place are 3 times as likely to be identified for special education."

Source --- Rhodes, Ochoa, Ortiz (the book is noted in the resources)

Given that most school districts hover between 12 and 15 percent of their total student population qualified for special education services, this would mean that within these district 36% to 45% of the language learners are also qualified as students with disabilities. Hopefully you read that and realized how crazy that is!

There is no group of students that exists that has a disability rate of 36% to 45%. I have worked with many districts where between 30 and 40 percent of their ELL qualified students are qualified for special education (meaning that someone, some team, said that each and every one of those children has a disability). In all of the districts I've worked with, except one, the teams and staff members had no idea this was occurring. The exceptions are the district in which they have been mandated training by the state.

This is not bad people purposefully doing things to harm children. These are good and caring people who need more knowledge, more options, and need to know their own data and the research around the choices that can be made for their students.

Answer to question number 2: Using the same list, which categories do you believe have very low rates of disproportionality? And, why?

The categories with the lowest disproportionality are: hearing impairment (including deafness), visual impairment (including blindness), orthopedic impairment, traumatic brain injury, deaf-blindness, and multiple disabilities.

The following is based upon working many years in this field and working with people across the country on these issues. Within each of these categories the student(s) present with something that is very concrete in nature, something that usually can be measured objectively. If a student has blindness, they have blindness no matter what language that they speak. Also, the majority of the students who qualify in these categories need special education services, regardless of the language they speak or do not yet speak. Therefore, the fact that they are a language learner is not a defining characteristic in the evaluation, but instead a consideration or factor.

Answer to question number 3: Why could it be valuable to know what category a student qualifies within and to know more about that category of eligibility?

Knowing the category in which the student is qualified helps the team to understand the root cause of the struggles that the student is facing. It is very easy to link blindness or deafness to struggles with reading, writing or math. However, it is far more difficult to understand the links of a specific learning disability to struggles in reading, writing or math. That is, the root cause of the disability is unknown and/or difficult to understand. As a teacher, though, knowing that a student has the health condition of ADHD and knowing the characteristics of ADHD helps in planning the environment and learning modules for the student. For example, the student might require small group or even 1-to-1 instruction to understand a concept, but once understood they are able to move forward quickly. In contrast, a student with a learning disability might need the teacher to present the material in many different ways and to repeat the teaching many times in order to understand the concepts. Usually, the forward progress for these students takes more repetition, more variety of strategies, and more time.

You might have noticed that a few categories were not discussed, like Other Health Impaired and Autism. The disproportionality in these categories varies greatly, sometimes with over qualification and sometimes with under qualification. Part of the problem could be parents who do not speak English have a more difficult time navigating our medical system to get a diagnosis, therefore the category of Other Health Impaired could be used less (a theory exists that some of those children are then just shifted to the Specific Learning Disability category, creating part of the over usage of this category with language learners). These areas are less consistent than the other areas.

Reflections

Now that you have read the introduction to this section, taken the quiz, and read the answers, it is time to reflect.

1) What have you learned that is new information to you?
2) How will this change your work with students moving forward?
3) What do you still need to learn? Where will you find it? When will you find it?

Question and Answer Section (Modules 3, 4 and 5)

Each of the following modules will contain a quiz, a section of questions and answers, and then a reflection section.

Questions from WABE Training

These questions were created by Steve by first asking a group of roughly 250 special education staff "What do you want ELL teachers to know about Special Education?" Then, Steve led a session at the Washington Association of Bilingual Educators 2014 state conference. During this session, Steve provided the teachers a brief summary of the information gained from the survey of the special education staff, followed by the ELL teachers asking and providing questions to Steve. Steve answered some of the questions both during the session and later in writing. This work was reviewed by many individuals across the state, including past board members from WABE (Washington Association of Bilingual Education) and WSASP (Washington State Association of School Psychologists) and staff members at OSPI (Office of Superintendent of Public Instruction). It is meant to help, but not supplant (instruction by your district or OSPI), given the individuality of situations you will encounter. You will need to discuss some of these questions and answers with individuals who are experts at interpreting the law within your district and within your state. The laws are interpreted differently at times.

Question and Answer - Module 3

The Referral Process

Step 1:

Take 15 minutes and write down the following:

1) What you know about the referral process?
2) What has been problematic or frustrating for you during the referral process?
3) What you think you need to learn more about regarding the referral process?

What does the legal process of becoming special education identified look like?

This is a topic that also could take a book! The OSPI Special Education website has a description of the process. In a nutshell, a referral is made. The referral process is a process in which a team gathers data (including parent input) to determine whether or not to propose a special education evaluation. If the team (best practice would include the ELL teacher if the student is ELL qualified) proposes to evaluate a student and the parent consents, then a team of people evaluate the student in all areas of concern. It is very important to be comprehensive and not only focus on the "obvious," but to keep an open mind to where the data and input leads the team during the evaluation. Once the evaluation work has been completed, the team (which includes the parent(s)) meets to discuss the data and information. The team is looking to see whether or not the data and information meets the criteria for one of the 14 categories outlined in the WAC (Washington Administrative Code), whether or not this disability is adversely impacting the student's access to their education, and whether or not the student needs special education and related services in order to address the adverse impact of the disability. If all of these are answered yes by the team, the team then knows (from the data, information, and discussion) the needs of the student and the student is qualified for special education services. Within 30 calendar days, an Individual Education Plan is written to address these needs.

OSPI has produced Technical Assistance Paper(s) (TAPs) over the years. This topic is addressed in TAP 1, and the following is a link to TAP 1.

http://k12.wa.us/SpecialEd/pubdocs/TAP1.pdf

Who can I contact if I have questions about tests or processes?

Your school psychologists and speech and language pathologists should be able to answer most or all of these questions. If they cannot answer your question, they should know who to ask. Do not give up, because your efforts could lead to new knowledge for many people involved.

When is it appropriate to refer an ELL student for special education?

It is appropriate when you believe that the student you are working with has a disability. However, please work with your teams to discuss this and work with your teams to make sure that people have truly examined the possibility that the student's deficits could be language learning. We have over identification in much higher numbers than under identification due to beliefs that cannot be validated through rigorous examination.

Do we wait for appropriate language acquisition?

We do not wait unless we believe that what we see is not related to a disability (based upon careful examination, data and strong processes). We could be wrong by waiting, but there is more over identification than under identification. The over identification tends to occur far more frequently in the categories of Specific Learning Disability, Speech or Language Impaired, and Developmentally Delayed. Many groups have under identification in the category of Other Health Impaired. Knowing this and your school and district data can help inform decision making. The goal is not over or under identification, but finding students who truly have disabilities, regardless of language learner status, whose disabilities are adversely impacting their education and who need specially designed instruction.

Staff have an obligation to refer a student for potential special education services once multi-tiered academic supports have been exhausted and the student is not making progress. Be sure to document the student's progress and bring evidence to the referral meeting. Please note, a referral cannot be delayed based upon a lack of intervention, but best practice is to attempt intervention first when it makes sense. For example, the majority of students with blindness need special education services (so, documented interventions prior to referral and/or evaluation are less critical in most cases). In contrast, many struggling students do not have a specific learning disability and response to intervention is critical in determining difference from disability.

At what point do you refer a child who is an ELL but not progressing like other ELLs?

This depends greatly upon the level of success the students in your school and district are having. The first step would be getting data from the state and your district regarding progress of ELLs in general. For example, at a state level, what is the average length of time ELLs stay at each language acquisition level and what are the average scores on your state and local testing? If you have this type of data, then you can compare this student against other students who are as similar as possible regarding linguistic history, educational background, and culture, and see whether or not the student you are concerned about is performing like other students in your school (then a referral would not be the focus in most cases) or is performing well below other students in your school (then a referral could be appropriate). There are a lot more issues that should be examined, and if your district does not already have a process in place that looks across students and schools and analyzes the many issues, then the ELL Critical Data Process could assist. In either case, use the discussions to better understand the needs of the student, then the team will know how to design the needed interventions.

When you are providing literacy instruction in their native language and they are not making progress how do you refer them?

All referrals are the same, whether ELL students or not. Whatever the process is in your building, follow it. Then, once the referral has begun, there are likely to be additional components for ELL students. The fact that they are getting native language instruction is very valuable. However, you will likely need to have data regarding how the instruction is working for ELLs in general in your building. Also, you will likely need to know many things about the history of this student (their educational history, how language is used in their home, sequential versus simultaneous bilingual, etc...) in order to make good decisions.

What are the data driven resources that prove kids need to be proficient in their native language first?

Students do not "need" to be proficient in their native language first, and some students may never reach a high level of proficiency in their native language, given their native language may fade away on them over time. However, the stronger the native language the more transferable skills. The work by Dr. Cummins, Dr. Catherine Collier, Dr. Virginia Collier and Dr. Thomas, and Dr. Grosjean are all examples that support this.

This comes down to what works on a systems level, and native language skills and/or support to increase those skills are widely proven to be a key to success for students in general.

How can we encourage districts to use 504 instead of sped maybe as an extension of RTI program?

Why would we do this? Section 504 is for students who have a disability and who need accommodations and/or modifications. Special education adds to this the need for specially designed instruction. Our goal is to find out what the needs are of the student, what services they qualify for, and help them to access those services. So, does your district have proportional or disproportional qualification rates? That is a place to begin.

Step 2:

Write down the following:

1) What do you now know about the referral process?
2) What is still problematic or frustrating for you during the referral process?
3) What is no longer problematic or frustrating for you regarding the referral process?

Question and Answer - Module 4

The Evaluation Process

Step 1:

Take 15 minutes and write down the following:

1) What you know about the evaluation process?
2) What has been problematic or frustrating for you during the evaluation process?
3) What you think you need to learn more about regarding the evaluation process?

How can I become conversant in testing terms and/or request other forms of tests or evidence?

Make some time to visit with your school psychologist and your speech and language pathologist. Ask them to show you some of the tests, and ask questions about those tests. This will likely lead to more questions. This is a journey that begins with curiosity. As you come across areas in which you have questions, ask your school psychologists and speech and language pathologists about good books and/or articles in the areas that make you most curious.

What do interpreters and school psychologists need to do to make sure that testing done in a language other than English is still valid and reliable?

Testing that is interpreted and/or translated is NOT reliable nor valid in the vast majority of the cases. However, it can be meaningful. For example, reading testing done in English on a student who does not speak English can provide a baseline for later comparison (nothing more). Reading testing done in the native language of the student can be analyzed against many factors to try to understand its meaning (e.g., how much exposure did the student have to reading in their native language and how does that compare to the results, how much did the interpreting and/or translating impact the structure of the test and therefore the meaning of the results, what is the rate of literacy in the target language….). The key to this is taking caution in analyzing the results of the testing and their potential meaning. When in doubt, do not place any significant meaning on the results.

At what point does culture influence eligibility for Sped Services?

Culture almost always impacts eligibility. There is very little work available on measuring acculturation, yet the law states we are supposed to take into account social and cultural issues. Measuring acculturation helps the evaluator understand potential impacts of culture on the testing, given that the tests are normed on students from the United States who have the average experience children have in our society. The key is trying to understand the impact, given their will be an impact. The work by Dr. Catherine Collier can be very helpful in this area.

How do you determine if it's a language barrier or a disability?

This is a very complex issue and the focus of Steve's three books, many books by Dr. Catherine Collier and books by Dr. Sam Ortiz. I cannot do this question justice in a few sentences. There are many, many questions to pose and answer in order to answer portions of this question, but I believe that reading the books noted in the resources can provide a great deal of information. Even with that, it takes a team of dedicated people working hard to make good decisions in this area based on student level evidence.

How do teachers get an IQ assessment done, so as to know a student's "ability" (not to qualify for Special Education, but to know if they aren't successful due to "lack of ability" or "lack of trying.")? Then, work on "Academics" or "Effort."

IQ testing is only done (with the exception of some districts that administer group IQ tests for Highly Capable/Gifted*) during the process of a special education evaluation. IQ tests are of extremely limited validity for language learners. The research over the past 100 years or so shows a very strong correlation between IQ scores and language acquisition level (meaning their ability to perform on the test changes greatly and not their innate ability). In a nutshell, it just would not work to answer this question.

On a personal note, I strongly believe that the vast majority of students who present as "lack of trying" are doing so out of a fear to try and/or confusion and not out of "laziness." Therefore, if we assume that we need to provide the student an avenue toward success, in place of "motivation," they are likely to find motivation due to success.

*Group IQ test results can provide lower scores than true ability for a multitude of reasons, yet high scores are likely to be more accurate given people cannot "fake" up.

How do we get the tests administered in the student's home language?

This can be done through the usage of an interpreter or via translation. However, staff need to understand that the standardization of the test and the design of the test might be destroyed through this action. Therefore, why is this being done? If the goal is to find baseline information for later comparison, it can be useful. If the goal is to make major decisions using this data, then a great deal of caution is needed and experts in the field are needed to help understand the true meaning of the test results.

Do we as teachers base it on learning disabilities versus physical and/or mental disabilities?

There needs to be a lot of discussion around this topic. The vast majority of disproportionality occurs in the categories of Learning Disabilities, Speech or Language Impairments, and Developmental Delays. We tend to have much better proportional identification in the other areas. Therefore, take more caution and examine things more closely in these categories. We tend to know that a student who has blindness or deafness needs help from special education services regardless of the language they speak. In contrast, we often identify students in the three noted categories without knowing the root cause of the concerns.

What culturally relevant IQ and/or academic testing are available?

Relevant is a difficult word in this context. Valid and reliable might be more accurate for this (given the answer is almost none). All IQ tests and academic tests have both cultural and linguistic loading, some just have less. The person who is administering these needs to research the work in this area to have a good understanding of the issues. The research can start with the work by Dr. Sam Ortiz. However, it should not stop there. Then, the question will remain, given the tools we have, how can we gain meaning out of the testing we have done?

What kind of tools/tests do you use and/or recommend for evaluating ELLs?

There are no tools that solve this challenge. Processes, strong processes, reduce the likelihood of inappropriate qualifications. These processes involve looking at the critical data, having the right people at the table (meaning people from across different groups) and having real discussions about whether the presenting problem is related to social, cultural, linguistic, experience or disability issues. This is difficult if people assume a deficit in a skill equals a disability.

I recommend the following books: Assessing Culturally and Linguistically Diverse Students, The ELL Critical Data Process, and Evaluating ELL Students for the Possibility of Special Education Qualification.

Can we use IQ tests from mother countries, and if so, would they be accepted?

If a student just arrived from another country, was formally educated in that country and there is a valid reason to believe a disability exists and you have a school psychologist who is bilingual (including the language in question), <u>you might be able to use that test</u>. In other words, probably not. It would not work. The norming of the assessment would make it impossible to know whether or not the student of concern had the correct experiences to perform in a reliable and valid manner on the test.

What support can we give to special education and ELL specialists when a child is misdiagnosed? The child is capable, but just struggles with language and goes to special education supports?

You need to provide proof. Provide any type of documentation that proves that the child is a capable learner. This could be report cards from a prior setting. This could be work that the child produces in their native language (that we have translated). Evidence of knowledge and learning capability is the key.

Step 2:

Write down the following:

1) What do you now know about the evaluation process?
2) What is still problematic or frustrating for you during the evaluation process?
3) What is no longer problematic or frustrating for you regarding the evaluation process?

Question and Answer - Module 5

Remaining Questions Across Multiple Topics:

Step 1:

First, read the following questions without reading the answers.

Then, take 15 minutes and write down the following:

1) What do you know about these topics?
2) What has been problematic or frustrating for you during these topics?
3) What do you think you need to learn more about regarding these topics?

How can a bilingual student who has been qualified for special education services receive appropriate services when the language of instruction in the special education classroom is English?

This is a great question, given people are struggling to try to find an answer to this that leads to good student outcomes. The reality is that this combination tends to lead to poor results. The research by Collier and Thomas shows that ELLs with disabilities are doing far better in Dual Language programs than the results of any study I have read regarding special education classroom outcomes in general. Native language support (the more the better if properly designed) is critical to student success. The books written by Collier and Thomas document their research (in which they analyzed more than 6,000,000 student files) in this area.

What language should be used if they qualify for special education services?

This depends greatly upon the student and the severity of their disability. If the student is communicating well in their native language, then native language support is very valuable. If the student is non-verbal or has very limited verbal abilities (e.g., less than 100 words used in their native language), then working on English with less native language support might make more sense. The team needs to work together, with multiple perspectives at the table (parents, general education, ELL, and special education) in order to best plan for each student individually.

Does an ELL student have to qualify for SLP in order to have language goals in their IEP?

Depends upon what you mean by language goals. All students who are dually qualified (ELL/Special Education) are to have their language learner needs considered when designing the IEP. However, for specific goals within the area of language (as an area of special education service), they would need to qualify for services from a Speech and Language Pathologist (which can be done as either Specially Designed Instruction or a Related Service). ELL-qualified students must also receive English language development (ELD) services. Best practice would be to include a description of the ELD services on the student's IEP.

For dual served students, what does it look like for LTELS (long-term ELLs) to exit?

The most recent "Dear Colleague" letter from the Department of Education made it clear that ALL students exit ELL services the same way, they test at a level on the ELPA-21 (an example of a state English language acquisition test) that indicates English language proficiency.

What role does trauma and its impact on brain development have on identifying/testing for a disability?

This is a topic of entire books and many research articles. Using Google Scholar can get you articles to read on the topic. There is research that indicates trauma has a negative impact on brain development. However, I fear that people read that and set low expectations of students who have been impacted by highly traumatic events. Students in trauma and who are living with the effects of trauma are more likely to be qualified for special education services, and sometimes those services are not meaningful in relationship to the student's needs. Please take each child one at a time and set high expectations that are supported within your school system.

How does trauma impact the rate of disability qualification?

Students living with the effects of trauma can present as having disabilities and therefore be qualified for services that may or may not be directly related to their needs. Qualification rates do not equal disability rates, or we would not have disproportionality.

How do we communicate with special education, ELL and general education teachers to make a team?

Most good teams have someone who takes a leadership role and helps to bring the team together in a productive manner. This person can be from any of these three groups. Also, sometimes there is a person much more willing to be the "voice" in helping to lead a group and someone else much more willing to be a strong supporter of the work. So, work with your colleagues from each of these groups to create a structure that leads to frequent, meaningful, and constructive dialogue. We all have something to add to the team.

How do we support the ELL needs of the students with severe disabilities who are served in self-contained classrooms?

This is a question in which an OSPI group and the BEAC are currently working on (these are groups in Washington who have created learning modules in this area that are posted to the OSPI website). There is not much literature in this area. As time moves forward, the goal of this group is to assist teachers around the state to best meet the needs of these students. Begin by collaborating with the special education teacher, as assistance and guidance on this topic is developed and shared.

How do we separate our behavior kids from true academic discrepancies?

Most school buildings, or at least most districts, have someone who is not just trained to complete Functional Behavioral Assessments, but is also good at doing it (and hopefully at providing support based upon the findings). In order to separate these issues we need someone on the team who is good at leading a team through a process like this. We are looking for things that are likely to predict the occurring behaviors and things that maintain these behaviors. Once we get a good handle on this, we are more likely to be able to understand the root causes of the behavior(s). And, more importantly, what we can provide an instruction(s) to lower the likelihood of the behavior occurring. We need to teach them skills, positive replacement behaviors, in order for them to be successful.

How do we work with school psychologists using examples rather than only numbers?

First, take a few minutes to sit down with them and discuss your concerns. Then, work together to determine the types of things that the team can work on to create the data needed to better understand the problems/concerns. If they are new to the profession or this is not an area of strength for them, expand the team (there is almost always someone within the school or district who can help make plans regarding the types and quality of evidence needed to have measurable data). Then, everyone involved can learn new skills.

How do you get to know the family if you cannot speak their language and they do not speak English?

First, you can invite them in for a meeting and have an interpreter to assist (interpreters for this purpose are paid through basic education funds. Ask your district for language access support for families). Second, you can work to find leaders in the community who function as cultural navigators and ask them to help. Third, you can use technology to help for smaller issues (this helps build the bond), like using iPhones or iPads and the voice program iTranslate.

I am sure others can add many items to this list, but this is a start.

Step 2:

Write down the following:

1) What did you learn that is new to you in this section?
2) How will that impact your work moving forward?
3) What do you think you need to learn more about regarding these topics?

Acronyms

The following is a list of acronyms commonly used in special within special education. You might want to keep a copy for later use. This was added to the self-directed learning because it might be a valuable resource in the future.

Acronym	Term
504 Plan	Section 504 of the Rehabilitation Act of 1973
AAC	Alternative Augmentative Communication
ABA	Applied Behavior Analysis
ABC	Antecedent, Behavior, Consequence
ADA	Americans with Disabilities Act
ADD	Attention Deficit Disorder
ADHD	Attention Deficit Hyperactivity Disorder
ADLs	Activities of Daily Living
AIM	Accessible Instructional Materials
APE	Adaptive Physical Education
APR	Annual Performance Report
ASD	Autism Spectrum Disorder
ASL	American Sign Language
AT	Assistive Technology
AYP	Annual Yearly Progress
B - 2	Birth through Two
BIP	Behavior Intervention Plan
CAP	Corrective Action Plan
CAPD	Central Auditory Processing Disorder
CD	Communication Disorder
CF	ChildFind
COTA	Certified Occupational Therapist Assistant
DB	Deaf-Blind
DD	Developmental Delay
DVR	Division of Vocational Rehabilitation
EBD	Emotional Behavior Disorder
ECSE	Early Childhood Special Education
ESY	Extended School Year
FAPE	Free Appropriate Public Education
FERPA	Family Educational Rights and Privacy Act
FBA	Functional Behavioral Assessment
GE	General Education
HI	Hearing Impaired
IA	Instruction Assistant
IAES	Interim Alternative Educational Setting
ID	Intellectual Disability

IDEA	Individuals with Disabilities Education Act
IEE	Independent Educational Evaluation
IEP	Individual Educational Plan
IHP	Individualized Health Plan
LD	Learning Disability
LEA	Local Education Agency
LRE	Least Restrictive Environment
MD	Multiple Disabilities
MDR	Manifestation Determination Review
MH	Multiple Handicapped
MOU	Memorandum of Understanding
NPS	Non-public School
OHI	Other Health Impairment
OI	Orthopedic Impairment
O & M	Orientation and Mobility
OSPI	Office of Superintendent of Public Instruction
OT	Occupational Therapist
PBIS	Positive Behavioral Interventions and Supports
PDD	Pervasive Developmental Disorder
PLAAFP	Present Level of Academic Achievement and Functional Performance
PT	Physical Therapy
PTA	Physical Therapy Assistant
PWN	Prior Written Notice
RTI	Response to Intervention
RS	Related Services
SAS	Supplementary Aids and Services
SDI	Specially Designed Instruction
SE or SpEd	Special Education
SEAC	Special Education Advisory Committee
SLD	Specific Learning Disorder
SLP	Speech Language Pathologist
SLPA	Speech Language Pathologist Assistant
SST	Student Support Team
TBI	Traumatic Brain Injury
TDD	Telecommunication Devices for the Deaf
VI	Visual Impairment

Scenarios (Modules 6, 7, and 8)

Module 6: Student struggling to learn to read, and speaks almost zero English outside the school setting

Module 7: Student struggling to learn to read, and speaks native language only with some relatives

Module 8: Student who has autism who happens to be an English language learner

Each of these is based upon a real situation, with the actual results. There was a lot more information available to the teams than presented here. The scenarios have limited information to allow you to process this without too many complications and within a reasonable amount of time.

Scenarios - Module 6

Student struggling to learn to read, and speaks almost zero English outside the school setting

You have several language learners in your classroom, but you are more concerned regarding one boy who is struggling to learn to read. In your school, you have an intervention teacher (system), and this student has been working within this system since kindergarten. He is now in 4th grade. He makes a lot of substitution errors, but your bigger concern is that he doesn't use context clues to understand some of the words or to be able to make inferences.

First questions:

What information should you gather if you want to talk with your building based team regarding this student?

What might you want to know more about in order to better understand this student?

Should you make a special education referral? If yes, why? If no, why not?

Go to the next page after creating your answers.

New information and your team meeting:

You were not sure about the information to gather, so you worked with the person who coordinates the meetings. From this, you learned to gather multiple work samples over time in the areas that you are concerned about. You read the student's cumulative file and took notes. You compiled information regarding how this student has progressed on the state language acquisition test.

You went to your team meeting, and people were impressed with what you brought to the meeting. However, there are still unanswered questions. For example, the team does not know if any English is spoken in the home or how the siblings of this student have performed in school.

Your team finds out the following information (in addition to the information you gathered):

You found out:

1) The work samples that you have clearly show that the student is not meeting the standards,
2) The student you are concerned about has made very slow progress on the state language acquisition test,
3) The cumulative file does show he has been in your school since kindergarten and all teacher reports indicate that he has consistently performed below standard, he has good attendance, and he has 3 siblings.

Your team does more investigating and finds the following information:

1) When compared to other language learners who speak the same language, his growth on the state language acquisition test is within that group,
2) When compared to his siblings, the performance is roughly the same for each of the sibling at the different grade levels.

What do you need to do next? Answer this question then go to the following page.

The next stage:

You hopefully said that you need to talk with the family to gather information and to express some concerns.

Upon talking with the family, you find out the following:

Outside the school setting this student spends very little time interacting with anyone who speaks English. The family has chosen to not allow the student to try to read in their native language, nor support him learning to read in their native language (they believed that he first needed to learn to read in English). The family is very supportive of any ideas that you have, but they will need to do everything in Spanish.

Where would you go from here (next steps)? After answering this question, go to the next page.

The "Results:"

The story above is a modified version of a real situation. This student, with the parent's permission and support, started working with the school psychologist (who happens to speak and read in Spanish) on reading in Spanish. The student was able to independently read grade level text in Spanish within about 6 weeks (mostly he just needed to learn some of the differences in pronunciation). The school psychologist learned that this student had much stronger day-to-day language skills in Spanish, but that all of his "CALP" was in English. This caused interesting problems for the student in reading in English, making the usage of contextual clues very difficult. The student quickly learned how to use contextual clues and make inferences in Spanish reading. The parents supported learning these skills, which the student then started to display in his English reading.

Reflection:

1) What can you take from this to your own work?
2) What might you do differently?
3) What would you do the same way?
4) What do you need to learn more about, after working through this?

Scenarios - Module 7

Student struggling to learn to read, and speaks native language only with some relatives

You have several language learners in your classroom, but you are more concerned regarding one who is struggling to learn to read. In your school, you have an intervention teacher (system), and this student has been working within this system since kindergarten. He is now in 4th grade. He makes a lot of substitution errors, but your bigger concern is that he doesn't use context clues to understand some of the words or to be able to make inferences.

Please note, this will have identical wording to Module 6 until the information section below. The two students happened to be in the same classroom.

First questions:

What information should you gather if you want to talk with your building based team regarding this student?

What might you want to know more about in order to better understand this student?

Should you make a special education referral? If yes, why? If no, why not?

Go to the next page after creating your answers.

New information and your team meeting:

You were not sure about the information to gather, so you worked with the person who coordinates the meetings. From this, you learned to gather multiple work samples over time in the areas that you are concerned about. You read the student's cumulative file and took notes. You compiled information regarding how this student has progressed on the state language acquisition test.

You went to your team meeting, and people were impressed with what you brought to the meeting. However, there are still unanswered questions. For example, the team does not know if any English is spoken in the home or how the siblings of this student have performed in school.

Your team finds out the following information (in addition to the information you gathered):

You found out:

1) The work samples that you have clearly show that the student is not meeting the standards,
2) The student you are concerned about has made very slow progress on the state language acquisition test,
3) The cumulative file does show he has been in your school since kindergarten and all teacher reports indicate that he has consistently performed below standard, he has good attendance, and he has 1 sibling.

Your team does more investigating and finds the following information:

1) When compared to other language learners who speak the same language, his growth on the state language acquisition test is below that of other students in your school,
2) When compared to his sibling, his performance is much lower. In fact, his second-grade sister is already reading at a higher level that he is reading.
3) His problem appears to be very specific to phonics/phoneme issues.

What do you need to do next? Answer this question then go to the following page.

The next stage:

You hopefully said that you need to talk with the family to gather information and to express some concerns.

Upon talking with the family, you find out the following:

The only people who the student speaks Spanish with are his mother and father; other relatives speak English primarily (but understand Spanish). His parents are very concerned about his progress, especially given that his little sister is already reading at a higher level than he is. They have worked with him on reading in Spanish, but he is demonstrating similar struggles. He just does not seem to be able to sound out words and he does not recognize very many words (sight vocabulary).

Where would you go from here (next steps)? After answering this question, go to the next page.

The "Results:"

The story above is a modified version of a real situation. In this case, the student was demonstrating a very specific concern (phonics/phoneme awareness struggles), his little sister (same environmental experiences) was already reading at a higher level (although 2 grade levels below him), he was demonstrating similar struggles in his native language, and his parents were very concerned regarding his learning.

The team determined that making a special education referral was a reasonable action and the parents provided permission to proceed with a special education evaluation. The student was determined to have a specific learning disability in reading. His math skills were well within the norm, and he demonstrated great math reasoning when the problems were read to him. Also, he demonstrated strong writing skills when spelling was not factored into the score.

Reflection:

1) What can you take from this to your own work?
2) What might you do differently?
3) What would you do the same way?
4) What do you need to learn more about, after working through this?

Scenarios - Module 8

Student who has autism who happens to be an English language learner

You have several language learners in your classroom, and the parents of one of your language learners tell you, "My son needs an IEP." The little boy has unusual behaviors and needs a lot of accommodations, but is performing at or above grade level in reading, math and written language.

First questions:

What information should you gather if you want to talk with your building based team regarding this student?

What might you want to know more about in order to better understand this student?

Should you make a special education referral? If yes, why? If no, why not?

Go to the next page after creating your answers.

New information and your team meeting:

You were not sure about the information to gather, so you went to visit with your school psychologist. You learned that the law requires that we process all special education referrals, and what the parent has stated constitutes a special education referral.

Your team finds out the following information.

1) The student has already been diagnosed with Autism by the local Children's Hospital,
2) The student has a lot of difficulties with effective communication and social interactions (you have been doing a great job of accommodating for this, and didn't see it as a problem/issue),
3) The file documents each teacher has had similar concerns.

What do you need to do next? Answer this question then go to the following page.

The next stage:

Given that this is now in the process of a special education referral, the school psychologist takes the lead in the situation. Your job at this point and time is to provide information to the school psychologist (and probably the Speech and Language Pathologist). The team now needs to gather information to determine whether there will be the proposal of an initial evaluation to the family or the refusal of an initial evaluation. Your state law will dictate the amount of time in which the team has in order to make this decision.

Where would you go from here (next steps)? After answering this question, go to the next page.

The "Results":

The story above is a modified version of a real situation. In most cases in which a student has Autism and the school can document a relationship of the autism to issue/concerns/problems within the school setting, the parents will be asked to provide their consent for an initial evaluation for the possibility of special education eligibility. The team did ask this parent for their consent and the parent granted their consent. The student was found eligible, given the direct relationship between his documented disability with one of the special education categories of eligibility, the documented relationship of this disability to an adverse impact on his access to his education, and that he needed special education services.

It is important to note that accessing education is not solely about reading, writing and math. Students can be successfully progressing from grade level to next grade level and still need special education services.

This student needed special education services for social skills development and services from a Speech and Language Pathologist for pragmatic language skills.

Reflection:

1) What can you take from this to your own work?
2) What might you do differently?
3) What would you do the same way?
4) What do you need to learn more about, after working through this?

Resources (books)

Dr. Catherine Collier

Separating Difference from Disability

Steve Gill and Ushani Nanayakkara

Special Education Referral or Not

The ELL Critical Data Process: Distinguishing between disability and language acquisition

Evaluating ELL Students for the Possibility of Special Education Qualification

Dr. Robert Rhodes, Dr. Salvador Hector Ochoa, and Dr. Samuel Ortiz

Assessing Culturally and Linguistically Diverse Students

Else Hamayan, Barbara Marler, and Jack Damico

Special Education Considerations for English Language Learners

Made in the USA
San Bernardino, CA
20 March 2018